— VISIT —
AMERICA'S
REGIONS!

Visit the SOUTHEAST

By Kathryn Walton

Enslow PUBLISHING

Please visit our website, www.enslow.com. For a free color catalog of all our high-quality books, call toll free 1-800-398-2504 or fax 1-877-980-4454.

Library of Congress Cataloging-in-Publication Data
Names: Walton, Kathryn, 1993- author.
Title: Visit the Southeast / Kathryn Walton.
Description: Buffalo, NY : Enslow Publishing, [2024] | Series: Visit America's regions | Includes bibliographical references and index.
Identifiers: LCCN 2023033345 (print) | LCCN 2023033346 (ebook) | ISBN 9781978537606 (library binding) | ISBN 9781978537590 (paperback) | ISBN 9781978537613 (ebook)
Subjects: LCSH: Southern States–Description and travel–Juvenile literature.
Classification: LCC F209.3 .W35 2024 (print) | LCC F209.3 (ebook) | DDC 917.5–dc23/eng/20230803
LC record available at https://lccn.loc.gov/2023033345
LC ebook record available at https://lccn.loc.gov/2023033346

Published in 2024 by
Enslow Publishing
2544 Clinton Street
Buffalo, NY 14224

Portions of this work were originally authored by Kathleen Connors and published as *Let's Explore The Southeast.* All new material in this edition is authored by Kathryn Walton.

Designer: Claire Wrazin
Editor: Natalie Humphrey

Photo credits: Series art (leather spine and corners) nevodka/Shutterstock.com, (map) Karin Hildebrand Lau/Shutterstock.com, (stamped boxes) lynea/Shutterstock.com, (old paper) Siam SK/Shutterstock.com, (vintage photo frame) shyshak roman/Shutterstock.com, (visitor's guide paper background) Andrey_Kuzmin/Shutterstock.com; cover, p. 1 (main) Anna Dunlop/Shutterstock.com; cover, p. 1 (inset) Dan Solomon/Shutterstock.com; pp. 5, 21 (map) pingebat/Shutterstock.com; p. 7 Michelle Yvonne Ouellette/Shutterstock.com; p. 9 anthony heflin/Shutterstock.com; p. 11 Malll Themd/Shutterstock.com; p. 13 (left) Tom Hirtreiter/Shutterstock.com, (right) f11photo/Shutterstock.com; p. 15 Ancha Chiangmai/Shutterstock.com; p. 17 Elena Veselova/Shutterstock.com; p. 18 File:Trail of tears map NPS.jpg/Wikimedia Commons; p. 19 JNix/Shutterstock.com.

Printed in the United States of America

CPSIA compliance information: Batch #CWENS24: For further information contact Enslow Publishing at 1-800-398-2504.

CONTENTS

Words in the glossary appear in **bold** type the first time they are used in the text.

WELCOME TO THE SOUTHEAST

The Southeast **region** of the United States is large! With many beaches, high mountains, and scenic hiking trails, it's a great place for every nature lover to explore. But nature isn't the only thing to see in the Southeast!

For anyone looking for history, the Southeast has many different historic spots to learn about. From places important to the **civil rights movement** to the birthplace of jazz and blues music, the sights of the Southeast shouldn't be missed!

• VISITOR'S GUIDE •

MARTIN LUTHER KING JR., ONE OF THE LEADERS OF THE CIVIL RIGHTS MOVEMENT, WAS BORN IN ATLANTA, GEORGIA. VISITORS TO ATLANTA CAN VISIT MARTIN LUTHER KING'S BIRTHPLACE!

This map shows the states that are commonly considered to be part of the Southeast.

THE BEST BEACHES

The southeastern United States is bordered by the Atlantic Ocean to the east and the Gulf of Mexico to the south and west. That means there's a lot of beaches! Places like the Outer Banks in North Carolina and Miami, Florida, are common vacation spots.

Many important bodies of water are found in the Southeast. The lower Mississippi River flows through Louisiana, Arkansas, Mississippi, Tennessee, and Kentucky. The Apalachicola River in Florida has some of the best fishing in the state!

• VISITOR'S GUIDE •

WHILE MANY STATES IN THE SOUTHEAST HAVE GREAT BEACHES, SOME STATES ARE LANDLOCKED. THIS MEANS THEY ARE NOT BORDERED BY THE OCEAN ON ANY SIDE. ARKANSAS, KENTUCKY, AND TENNESSEE ARE LANDLOCKED STATES.

Many visitors to the Outer Banks take tours to see wild horses!

A VISIT TO THE MOUNTAINS

Some of the best hiking and camping in the United States is found in the Appalachian Mountains. This mountain range cuts through the Southeast. The Appalachians include the Blue Ridge Mountains found in parts of South Carolina, Georgia, and other states.

In Crater of **Diamonds** State Park in Arkansas, you can dig for real diamonds! Visitors are allowed to keep any rock, **mineral**, or gemstone they dig up. More than 35,000 diamonds have been found by park visitors!

The Blue Ridge Parkway is about 469 miles (755 km) long.

• VISITOR'S GUIDE •

BLUE RIDGE PARKWAY IS A POPULAR PATH FOR SOUTHEASTERN APPALACHIAN ROAD TRIPS. IT RUNS BETWEEN SHENANDOAH NATIONAL PARK IN VIRGINIA AND GREAT SMOKY MOUNTAINS NATIONAL PARK IN NORTH CAROLINA AND TENNESSEE.

WARM WEATHER

The weather of the Southeast region is affected by the Gulf of Mexico, the Atlantic Ocean, and the Appalachian Mountains. States with coastal areas, such as Georgia, commonly have warm temperatures year-round. The mountains block cool air, while the Atlantic Gulf Stream brings in warm air.

Inland, summers can be even hotter. Alabama sometimes has temperatures nearing 100°F (38°C) during the summer. However, states that are more north or higher in the mountains can have snow during the winter!

Warm, sunny weather in states like Florida means many fruits and vegetables grow year-round!

• VISITOR'S GUIDE •

THE GULF STREAM IS A STRONG OCEAN CURRENT THAT BRINGS WARM WATER INTO THE ATLANTIC OCEAN FROM THE GULF OF MEXICO.

THE BIGGEST CITIES

There's a lot to do in the Southeast's biggest cities! The most populated city in the Southeast today, Jacksonville, Florida, was settled in 1822. It's named after President Andrew Jackson, who was the area's governor for a short time. Visitors can stop by the Jacksonville Historical Society to learn more.

The second-largest city in the Southeast is Charlotte, North Carolina. Visitors can stop by the NASCAR Hall Of Fame to learn about car racing and the people who made the sport what it is today.

• VISITOR'S GUIDE •

CHARLOTTE WAS NAMED AFTER ENGLAND'S QUEEN CHARLOTTE (1744–1818). THIS CITY IS SOMETIMES CALLED THE QUEEN CITY OF THE SOUTH BECAUSE OF THIS!

CHARLOTTE, NORTH CAROLINA

At Charlotte Douglas International Airport, visitors can see a statue of Queen Charlotte.

THE MUSIC SCENE

The Southeast is well known for its music scene! Memphis, Tennessee, is called the birthplace of blues and rock and roll. Visitors can stop by historic Beale Street for live music daily and many music **festivals**.

New Orleans, Louisiana, is the birthplace of jazz music. Atlanta, Georgia, is sometimes called the hip-hop capital of the United States! Visitors can check out art pieces showing the faces of famous hip-hop artists there.

• VISITOR'S GUIDE •

LOUIS ARMSTRONG, A JAZZ SINGER AND TRUMPET PLAYER, WAS BORN IN NEW ORLEANS. HE IS ONE OF THE MOST IMPORTANT FIGURES IN JAZZ MUSIC.

About 475,000 people visited the Jazz & **Heritage** Festival in New Orleans in 2022.

SOUL FOOD

Food is important to the people of the Southeast. From jambalaya in Louisiana to barbecue in Memphis, Tennessee, this region's food draws from French, West African, and Native American heritage, and more! It also draws from the region's local **agriculture** and seafood **industries**.

Soul food is another part of southern cooking. This style of food was created by formerly enslaved people and spread around the South after the Civil War. Today, most cities in the Southeast (and other regions) have soul food restaurants.

• VISITOR'S GUIDE •

IF YOU'RE IN CHARLESTON, SOUTH CAROLINA, YOU WON'T WANT TO MISS RODNEY SCOTT'S WHOLE HOG BBQ! RODNEY SCOTT IS A BARBECUE PITMASTER AND ONE OF THE FEW PITMASTERS TO WIN A JAMES BEARD AWARD, A GREAT HONOR IN THE FOOD WORLD.

There are many different styles of barbecue found in the Southeastern states. They use different meats, sauces, and seasonings!

THE TRAIL OF TEARS

The Trail of Tears National Historic Trail is another important stop for Southeast visitors. Many Native American groups once lived in the Southeast, including the Choctaw, Cherokee, and Seminoles.

The U.S. government forced many members of these groups and others from their homes and made them walk for thousands of miles. Visitors can walk parts of this same 5,043-mile (8,114 km) path in memory of the thousands of Native Americans who died on this journey.

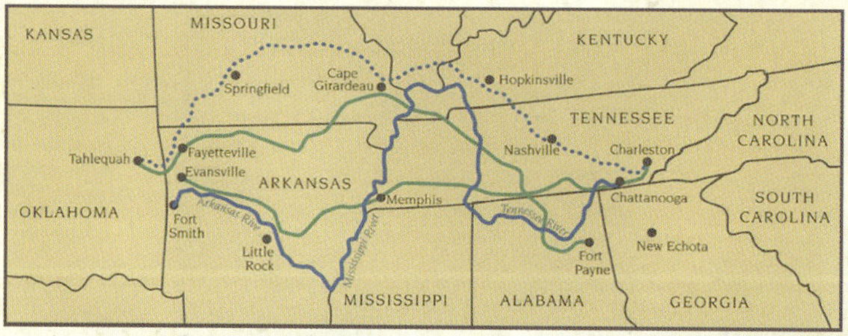

TRAIL OF TEARS NATIONAL HISTORIC TRAILS

The Cherokee people fought the U.S. government to keep their land for years.

• VISITOR'S GUIDE •

IN 1830, CONGRESS PASSED THE INDIAN REMOVAL ACT. THIS ACT LET THE GOVERNMENT FORCE NATIVE AMERICANS TO GIVE UP LAND. THEY HAD TO LIVE ON RESERVATIONS, OR LAND SET ASIDE BY THE U.S. GOVERNMENT FOR THE NATIVE GROUPS.

FAMOUS FACES

Many famous people were born in the Southeast! Presidents Andrew Jackson and James K. Polk were born in the Carolinas, and Bill Clinton was born in Arkansas. The actor Morgan Freeman was born in Memphis, Tennessee.

Whether it's a visit to one of the many historic places or a long drive down Blue Ridge Parkway, the many things to do and see in the Southeast make it a great region to explore!

• VISITOR'S GUIDE •

TODAY, YOU CAN VISIT CLINTON'S PRESIDENTIAL LIBRARY IN LITTLE ROCK, ARKANSAS, OR PRESIDENT JIMMY CARTER'S PRESIDENTIAL LIBRARY IN ATLANTA, GEORGIA.

MORE THINGS TO SEE IN THE SOUTHEAST

Check out more places to stop on your trip through the Southeast!

BILTMORE ESTATE

Stop by Asheville, North Carolina, to see the largest home in the United States.

DISCOVERY PLACE SCIENCE

This science museum in Charlotte, North Carolina, is made for guests to get hands-on with their learning!

THE SOUTHERN FOOD & BEVERAGE MUSEUM

Stop by New Orleans, Louisiana, to explore the history of food in the United States and give some new recipes a try.

THE FLORIDA AQUARIUM

This aquarium in Tampa, Florida, works not only to share animals with guests but also to keep **coral** and wild sea turtles safe.

GLOSSARY

agriculture: The science or job of farming.

civil rights movement: A time period in U.S. history starting in the 1950s in which Black Americans fought for equal civil rights, or the freedoms granted to us by law.

coral: A hard material found at the bottom of sea, made of the skeletons of small sea creatures.

diamond: A clear stone made of carbon. Often used to make jewelry.

festival: A public event usually hosted every year to celebrate something.

heritage: Something that comes from past members of a family or group.

industry: Businesses that produce goods in an area.

mineral: Matter in the ground that forms rocks.

region: A large area of land that has features that make it different from nearby areas of land.

FOR MORE INFORMATION

Books

Buckley, James. *New Orleans.* Charleston, South Carolina: Arcadia Children's Books, 2022.

Morris, Heather C. *The Climate Crisis in the Southeast.* Lake Elmo, Minnesota: Focus Readers, 2024.

Websites

Britannica Kids: Florida
www.kids.britannica.com/kids/article/Florida/345469
Learn more about how Florida became a state and discover more facts about it.

National Geographic Kids: Native People of the American Southeast
www.kids.nationalgeographic.com/history/article/native-people-of-the-american-southeast
Learn more about the Native Americans who lived and still live in the Southeast region.

Publisher's note to educators and parents: Our editors have carefully reviewed these websites to ensure that they are suitable for students. Many websites change frequently, however, and we cannot guarantee that a site's future contents will continue to meet our high standards of quality and educational value. Be advised that students should be closely supervised whenever they access the internet.

INDEX